D1219539

World of Mammals

Zebras

by Wendy Perkins

Consultant:
Suzanne B. McLaren
Collection Manager, Section of Mammals
Carnegie Museum of Natural History
Edward O'Neil Research Center
Pittsburgh, Pennsylvania

Mankato, Minnesota

Bridgestone Books are published by Capstone Press,
151 Good Counsel Drive, P.O. Box 669, Mankato, Minnesota 56002.
www.capstonepress.com

Library of Congress Cataloging-in-Publication Data
Perkins, Wendy, 1957–
      Zebras / by Wendy Perkins.
      p. cm.—(Bridgestone books. World of mammals)
      Includes bibliographical references and index.
      ISBN 0-7368-3722-1 (hardcover)
      1. Zebras—Juvenile literature. I. Title. II. Series: World of mammals.
QL737.U62P47 2005
599.665'7—dc22   2004015229

Summary: A brief introduction to zebras, discussing their characteristics, habitat, life cycle, and
      predators. Includes a range map, life cycle illustration, and amazing facts.

Editorial Credits
Erika L. Shores, editor; Molly Nei, set designer; Ted Williams, book designer; Erin Scott, Wylde Hare
      Creative, illustrator; Kelly Garvin, photo researcher; Scott Thoms, photo editor

Photo Credits
Brand X Pictures/John Lambert, 1
Craig Brandt, 4, 6, 20
Getty Images Inc./S. Purdy Matthews, cover
McDonald Wildlife Photography/Joe McDonald, 16
Minden Pictures/Mitsuaki Iwago, 18
Robin Brandt, 12
Tom & Pat Leeson, 10

1 2 3 4 5 6 10 09 08 07 06 05

Table of Contents

Zebras

Zebras are African animals known for their black and white stripes. While zebras are not horses, they are part of the horse family. Zebras, horses, and donkeys are **mammals**. Mammals are **warm-blooded** and have backbones. Female mammals feed milk to their young.

Three types of zebras live in Africa. Plains zebras are the heaviest of all zebras. Grevy's zebras are the tallest. Mountain zebras are the smallest.

◄ Most zebras in Africa are plains zebras.

What Zebras Look Like

Like horses, zebras have long faces and legs. A zebra's stripes make it unique. No two zebras have exactly the same stripe pattern.

Zebras have short manes and long tails. A zebra's mane sticks up from the back of its neck. Black and white hair grows on a zebra's tail.

Each type of zebra has different ears. Grevy's zebras have large, round ears. Mountain zebras' ears are long. Plains zebras have smaller ears than the other types.

◄ Each zebra has a unique pattern of black and white stripes.

Zebras Range Map

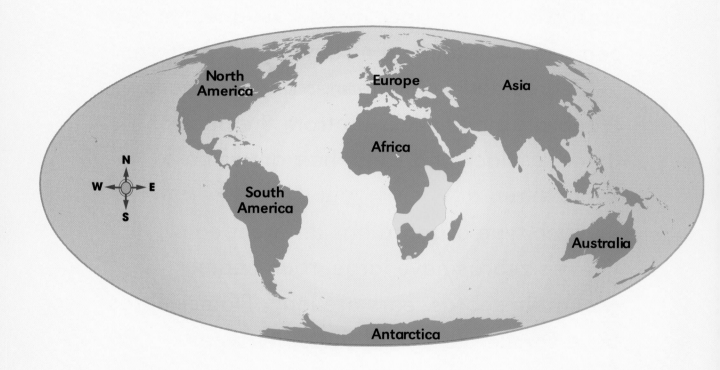

North America

Europe

Asia

Africa

South America

N
W · E
S

Australia

Antarctica

Where Zebras Live

Zebras in the World

Zebras are found only in Africa. Plains zebras live in the eastern and southwestern parts of Africa. Grevy's zebras are found only in northern Kenya and southern parts of Ethiopia. Mountain zebras live on the southwest edge of Africa. They are found in the mountains of Angola, Namibia, and South Africa.

◄ Zebras live only in Africa.

Zebra Habitats

Most zebras live in open, grassy **habitats**. Plains zebras live in wet **savannas**. These grasslands receive a great deal of rain. Grevy's zebras live in dry savannas where little rain falls.

Mountain zebras live on mountain slopes. They have narrow hooves that help them walk on mountain trails.

◀ Plains zebras graze on savannas where rain falls.

What Zebras Eat

Zebras move all day in search of grass. Antelope usually **graze** with zebras. A zebra only eats the top part of the grass. It is the toughest part of a blade of grass. A zebra's sharp front can teeth easily bite it off. Antelope eat the grass that is left behind by zebras.

If there is no grass to eat, zebras munch leaves from bushes. Some zebras even nibble on bark.

◀ Grevy's zebras spend more than half the day eating.

The Life Cycle of a Zebra

Newborn foal

6-month-old foal

1-year-old

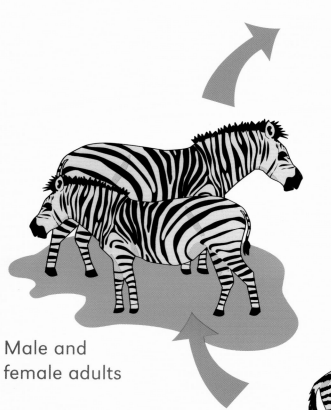

Male and
female adults

Producing Young

Zebras live together in **herds**. A herd usually has one male, one to six females, and their young. Female zebras are called mares. Male zebras are stallions. The oldest mare leads the group.

A mare usually **mates** only with the herd's stallion. About one year later, a young zebra called a foal is born. The mare moves away from the herd to give birth. After the foal is born, the mare licks it clean and pushes it to stand.

Growing Up

Newborn foals have brown stripes. The stripes turn black as the foal gets older.

Soon after it is born, a zebra foal is strong enough to run. It stays close to its mother as she grazes. If a **predator** comes near, all the foals stay safe in the middle of the herd.

Foals drink milk from their mothers for about one year. They also eat grass.

◀ A zebra foal stands soon after it is born.

Dangers to Zebras

Zebras must stay alert to danger. Hyenas and wild dogs hunt zebras. Big cats, such as lions and leopards, also hunt zebras.

When a predator charges a herd, the zebras run close together. Their moving stripes can confuse a predator. Zebras will also fight to protect the herd. A stallion will kick a predator to scare it away.

Zebras face dangers every day. But zebras are good at defending themselves. Zebras will continue to graze in Africa for years to come.

◄ Zebras run fast to escape lions and other predators.

Amazing Facts about Zebras

- Some zebras have shadow stripes. These yellow or gray stripes are between the black stripes.
- Zebras can run as fast as 40 miles (64 kilometers) per hour. The world's fastest animal, the cheetah, can run at speeds of about 70 miles (113 kilometers) per hour.
- Zebras live for about 18 to 25 years.
- At night, zebras take turns sleeping. One zebra stays awake to warn the herd when a predator is near.

◄ Even zebra foals can have shadow stripes. These zebras have gray or yellow stripes between their black stripes.

Glossary

graze (GRAYZ)—to eat grass or other plants on the ground

habitat (HAB-uh-tat)—the place and natural conditions where an animal lives

herd (HURD)—a large group of animals that live together

mammal (MAM-uhl)—a warm-blooded animal that has a backbone; female mammals feed milk to their young.

mate (MAYT)—to join together to produce young

predator (PRED-uh-tur)—an animal that hunts other animals for food

savanna (suh-VAN-uh)—a large, flat area of grassland

warm-blooded (warm-BLUHD-id)—having a body temperature that stays the same

Read More

Murray, Julie. *Zebras.* A Buddy Book. Edina, Minn.:
Abdo, 2003.

Whitehouse, Patricia. *Zebra.* Heinemann Read and Learn.
Chicago: Heinemann Library, 2003.

Internet Sites

FactHound offers a safe, fun way to find
Internet sites related to this book. All of
the sites on FactHound have been
researched by our staff.

Here's how:
1. Visit *www.facthound.com*
2. Type in this special code **0736837221** for
   age-appropriate sites. Or enter a search word
   related to this book for a more general search.
3. Click on the **Fetch It** button.

FactHound will fetch the best sites for you!

Index